Expressions
of
Thanksgiving

Emily and Daniel Myers

Illustrated by Daniel Myers

ISBN 979-8-88832-194-2 (paperback)
ISBN 979-8-88832-562-9 (hardcover)
ISBN 979-8-88832-195-9 (digital)

Christian Faith Publishing
832 Park Avenue
Meadville, PA 16335
www.christianfaithpublishing.com

All scriptures are taken from the King James Bible.
Hymn or song information is from Hymnary.org

Illustrated by Daniel Myers

Printed in the United States of America

Dear family and friends,

This year has been difficult in many ways for many reasons, and even now, we are entering more uncertain times as we write this one week before the 2020 presidential election.

Now more than ever seems a good time to spend a little extra time giving thanks to God. It seems Thanksgiving time is often so busy, and we have so little time to really reflect as much as we ought on God's goodness!

We want our children to grow up being thankful and also learning not only our history of God's providence and our Thanksgiving traditions but also the great hymns and Bible verses of thankfulness to God, so we have compiled this little book for our own use and would like to share it with you. It is meant to be used in the weeks leading up to and possibly a few days after our Thanksgiving holiday.

Each part is divided into six daily readings, and each part has a thanksgiving hymn to practice learning, as well as a thanksgiving children's song, a thanksgiving psalm and memory verse, a special *turkey* recipe, and a little activity. Of course, you can do just part.

May God bless you all this Thanksgiving season.

–Daniel and Emily Myers
Evaleah, Danny, Loralee, Emybelle, Sarabella, and Peter

Contents

Part 1

Make Ready for Thanksgiving!

Part 1 Hymn Highlight

Come, Ye Thankful People, Come

Come, ye thankful people, come, raise the song of harvest home; all is safely gathered in, ere the winter storms begin; God our Maker doth provide for our wants to be supplied; come to God's own temple, come, raise the song of harvest home.

All the world is God's own field, fruit as praise to God we yield; wheat and tares together sown are joy or sorrow grown; first the blade and then the ear, then the full corn shall appear; Lord of harvest, grant that we wholesome grain and pure may be.

For the Lord our God shall come, and shall take the harvest home; from the field shall in that day all offenses purge away, giving angels charge at last in the fire the tares to cast; but the fruitful ears to store in the garner evermore.

Even so, Lord, quickly come, bring thy final harvest home; gather thou thy people in, free from sorrow, free from sin, there, forever purified, in thy presence to abide; come, with all thine angels come, raise the glorious harvest home. (Henry Alford (1844), public domain)

Short Chorus or Children's Song

Thank Him, Thank Him

> Thank Him, Thank Him all ye little children
> God is love; God is love
> Thank Him, Thank Him all ye little children
> God is love; God is love. (Anonymous, public domain)

Psalm Highlight

Psalm 107:1–32

O give thanks unto the LORD, for he is good: for his mercy endureth for ever.

Let the redeemed of the LORD say so, whom he hath redeemed from the hand of the enemy;

And gathered them out of the lands, from the east, and from the west, from the north, and from the south.

They wandered in the wilderness in a solitary way; they found no city to dwell in.

Hungry and thirsty, their soul fainted in them.

Then they cried unto the LORD in their trouble, and he delivered them out of their distresses.

And he led them forth by the right way, that they might go to a city of habitation.

Oh that men would praise the LORD for his goodness, and for his wonderful works to the children of men!

For he satisfieth the longing soul, and filleth the hungry soul with goodness.

Such as sit in darkness and in the shadow of death, being bound in affliction and iron;

Because they rebelled against the words of God, and contemned the counsel of the most High:

Therefore he brought down their heart with labour; they fell down, and there was none to help.

Then they cried unto the LORD in their trouble, and he saved them out of their distresses.

He brought them out of darkness and the shadow of death, and brake their bands in sunder.

Oh that men would praise the LORD for his goodness, and for his wonderful works to the children of men!

For he hath broken the gates of brass, and cut the bars of iron in sunder.

Fools because of their transgression, and because of their iniquities, are afflicted.

Their soul abhorreth all manner of meat; and they draw near unto the gates of death.

Then they cry unto the LORD in their trouble, and he saveth them out of their distresses.

He sent his word, and healed them, and delivered them from their destructions.

Oh that men would praise the LORD for his goodness, and for his wonderful works to the children of men!

And let them sacrifice the sacrifices of thanksgiving, and declare his works with rejoicing.

They that go down to the sea in ships, that do business in great waters;

These see the works of the LORD, and his wonders in the deep.

For he commandeth, and raiseth the stormy wind, which lifteth up the waves thereof.

They mount up to the heaven, they go down again to the depths: their soul is melted because of trouble.

They reel to and fro, and stagger like a drunken man, and are at their wit's end.

Then they cry unto the LORD in their trouble, and he bringeth them out of their distresses.

He maketh the storm a calm, so that the waves thereof are still.

Then are they glad because they be quiet; so he bringeth them unto their desired haven.

Oh that men would praise the LORD for his goodness, and for his wonderful works to the children of men!

Let them exalt him also in the congregation of the people, and praise him in the assembly of the elders.

Key Verses
(Psalms 107:8, 15, 21, and 31)

Oh that men would praise the LORD for his goodness, and for his wonderful works to the children of men!

Featured Turkey Recipe
Simple Fruit Salad Turkeys

You will need the following ingredients:

> Fresh pineapple cut into rings
> Red and green grapes—washed
> Oranges—whole peeled (reserve some peel for decoration)
> Whole cloves for eyes
> Toothpicks

Using the sketch as a guide. Use toothpicks to hold the orange and pineapple ring together and stick on the grape feathers and head. Push the pointed end of the clove into head grape for the eyes. Cut a piece of orange peel for the beak and cut the grapes or peel for the feet. Use as decoration on the dinner table and then enjoy!

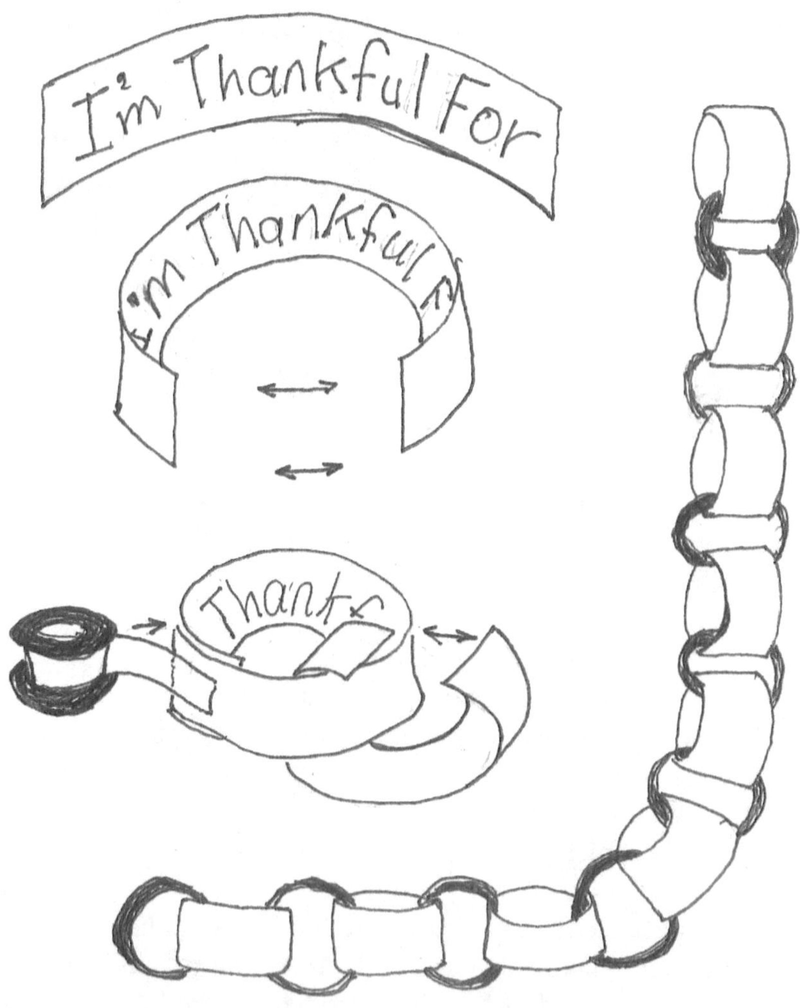
I'm Thankful For
I'm Thankful For
I'm Thankful
Thanks

Part 1 Activity
Thankfulness Chain

The materials needed:

1. Construction or other (preferably fall colors) paper
2. Scissors or paper cutter
3. Staples, glue, or tape

Cut strips of paper approximately 1.5 inches wide.

Each family member writes something they are thankful for on two to four strips. Then take the strips and loop them together to make a chain. Every day or several times throughout this part or even until Thanksgiving Day, try to write something you are thankful for and add another chain. Use to decorate your house. On Thanksgiving Day, take the chain down and divide it among members of the family to read. Someone could go through them and make stacks of duplicates if there are lots of chains to save time.

Suggestion: Each time a child grumbles, they have to think of something to be thankful for in this situation and add another link.

Day 1

When you hear about Thanksgiving Day, what is your first thought? Big family gatherings? Turkey? Cooking in a hot kitchen? Fall colors and pilgrims? Dread of the piles of dirty dishes and leftovers to clean up? Or is your first thought of how blessed you are and, more importantly, of our heavenly Father, who has given us all good things to enjoy?

You can be thankful for something to a certain extent without being thankful to God. Still, the roots of our national holiday, Thanksgiving Day, are most certainly to give thanks specifically to God Almighty—to Jesus Christ—for his provision and care for us. Thanksgiving Day is probably the least commercialized of our major holidays. Because of this association with thanking God specifically, there are those now who try to refer to the holiday as Turkey Day to further remove thoughts of God.

Although we hopefully do not like how much our society has tried to remove God from all areas, including Thanksgiving Day, how often do we—in all the hustle and bustle of getting ready for Thanksgiving Day—forget to be as truly thankful as we ought to our gracious God for all he has done? To give thanks, well, it is good to have an understanding of what *thanksgiving* means. According to *Noah Webster's 1828 Dictionary, thanksgiving* means rendering or the act of rendering thanks or expressing gratitude for good received, favors, or mercies.

A public celebration of divine goodness;
also, a day set apart for religious services, specially
to acknowledge the goodness of God, either in
any remarkable deliverance from calamities or

danger, or in the ordinary dispensation of his
bounties.

To be *thankful* is to show appreciation. It is an acknowledgment
of gratefulness: to show gratitude, to be indebted to, and to bless.

In the Bible (KJV), although the actual word *thanksgiving* is only
seen thirty times, the concept of thanksgiving with various words is
seen well over one hundred times in the Old Testament and over sev-
enty in the New Testament. In both Old and New Testaments, there
are a number of root words used to convey the idea of giving thanks.

The most often used word in the Old Testament is the Hebrew
word *ydh,* defined as acknowledging what is right about God in praise
and thanksgiving (as in 1 Chronicles 16:34); it is a right acknowledgment of self before God in confessing sin.

In the New Testament, the word most used is the Greek word
eucharisteo, meaning: to be grateful, to feel thankful, to give thanks,
to actively express gratitude [toward], to say grace, and to give thanks
with joy!

Make this thanksgiving season a true season of joyful thankfulness to God!

Enter into his gates with thanksgiving, and into his courts
with praise: be thankful unto him, and bless his name.

—Psalm 100:4

Day 2

On October 3, 1789, our first president—George Washington—issued a national day of thanksgiving proclamation in the United States.

It reads in part:

> Whereas it is the duty of all Nations to acknowledge the providence of Almighty God, to obey his will, to be grateful for his benefits, and humbly to implore his protection and favor… [*I*] recommend to the People of the United States a day of public thanksgiving and prayer to be observed by acknowledging with grateful hearts

the many signal favors of Almighty God especially by affording them an opportunity peaceably to establish a form of government for their safety and happiness.

Now therefore I do recommend and assign Thursday the 26th day of November next to be devoted by the People of these States to the service of that great and glorious Being, who is the beneficent Author of all the good that was, that is, or that will be—That we may then all unite in rendering unto him our sincere and humble thanks—for his kind care and protection of the People of this Country previous to their becoming a Nation—for the signal and manifold mercies, and the favorable interpositions of his Providence which we experienced in the course and conclusion of the late war…and also that we may then unite in most humbly offering our prayers and supplications to the great Lord and Ruler of Nations and beseech him to pardon our national and other transgressions—to enable us all, whether in public or private stations, to perform our several and relative duties properly and punctually—to render our national government a blessing to all the people, by constantly being a Government of wise, just, and constitutional laws, discreetly and faithfully executed and obeyed—to protect and guide all Sovereigns and Nations (especially such as have shewn kindness unto us) and to bless them with good government, peace, and concord—To promote the knowledge and practice of true religion and virtue, and the encrease of science among them and us—and generally to grant unto all Mankind such a degree of temporal prosperity as he alone knows to be best.

This was Washington's first proclamation as president of the United States, but many times as general, he had exhorted a time of prayer, fasting, and thanksgiving, including setting aside December 18, 1777, after the victory at Saratoga.

We are blessed to live in a nation that has acknowledged God's providential hand in leading and guiding our nation in its thanksgiving traditions.

> And let them sacrifice the sacrifices of thanksgiving,
> and declare his works with rejoicing.

—Psalm 107:22

16   EMILY AND DANIEL MYERS

Day 3

"O give thanks unto the Lord; for his: for his mercy endureth forever," so joyfully begins Psalm 136!

The first three and also the last verse all begin with "O give thanks" and imply that each one is meant to be read as if it also begins with *O give thanks*. Another thing that makes this beautiful psalm stand out is all twenty-six verses end in the same refrain "for his mercy endureth forever."

Mercy is forgiveness, divine love for the wrongdoer, gentle treatment. How wonderful is God's mercy toward us that lasts not just for today or for this time in our lives, and no, not just for those who have gone before us, but forever—from the beginning of time and with no end.

With the psalmist, we give thanks to God because of the following reasons:

> He is good.
> He is the God of gods.
> He is the Lord of lords.
> He alone does great wonders.
> His wisdom made the heavens.
> He created our world.
> He made the great lights.
> He made our sun, not just for light but for warmth and more.
> He gave us the moon to rule the night.
> He smote Egypt with plagues.
> He brought his people in Israel out from Egypt.
> He showed his power—strong hands and stretched out arms.

He divided the Red Sea in two parts.
He made Israel to pass through on dry ground.
He drowned the Pharaoh and his army in the sea.
He led his people through the wilderness.
He subdued great kings—he is able.
He slew famous kings—nothing is too hard for God.
He slew Sihon, king of the Amorites—he knows even our enemies by name.
He slew Og, the king of Bashan—the times of all are in his hands.
He gave his land for a heritage.
He gave it to Israel.
He remembered us in our lowly (sinful) state.
He rescued us from our enemies (chiefly from Satan) when he gave Jesus, who died and rose again.
He gives us food and all the good things we enjoy.
He *is* the God of heaven—there is no other name under heaven given among men whereby we might be saved!

We give thanks, and as we look back and see how he has shown his mercy in the past to his people, we can be confident that he will continue. He did not just tell us that his mercy endures forever, but he has shown us throughout history, even until this present time. And because he has said it endures forever, we know that it will continue to be shown to those who are his own without end.

As we look at what *mercy* is, we remember God's greatest act of mercy toward us when he sent his Son—Jesus—who was without sin to die on the cross, paying the price for our sins, that whosoever believeth in him should not perish, but should obtain mercy and forgiveness and should have everlasting life!

> O give thanks unto the God of heaven:
> for his mercy endureth forever.
>
> —Psalm 136:26

Day 4

And let the peace of God rule in your hearts, to the which
also ye are called in one body; and be ye thankful.

—Colossians 3:15

In the Old Testament, one of the sacrifices that the Israelites could make was a thanksgiving offering. Actually, the first time we see the word *thanksgiving* in the Bible is in reference to a *thanksgiving offering*. Thanksgiving offerings were a type of peace offering.

Just three of the interesting things we bring out about the thanksgiving offering in Leviticus 7 are the following:

1. The thanksgiving offering was to be offered not just with unleavened bread but also with leavened bread. There is only one other offering—first fruits—where leavened

bread is to be presented to God. As leaven often represents sin in the Bible, this offering of thanksgiving with both unleavened and leavened bread can remind us that we are to thank God for all things he brings into our lives—both the good and the bad.

2. The thanksgiving offering was to be eaten by all, not wholly burnt as some or eaten just by the priest as others, but to be shared by both the priest's families and the family that gave the offering. The thanksgiving offering brought people together in a feast of Thanksgiving to God and in thanking God, closer to him as well.

3. The thanksgiving offering was all to be eaten that same day—none of it left until the morning. We ought to offer our thanks to God every day—not try to rely on yesterday's offering of thanks. Each day is a new day. God's mercies are new every morning, and our Thanksgiving should be offered up every day.

By him therefore let us offer the sacrifice of praise to God continually, that is, the fruit of our lips giving thanks to his name.

—Hebrews 13:15

Day 5

So far, we have looked at giving thanks from a few different angles. Today, we want to look just a little at the other side—that of receiving or expecting thanks. While we ought to always thank God and the people around us who have done things for us, we should not be doing things to receive thanks or in expectation of thanks, as stated in Colossians 3:23 and 24, "And whatsoever ye do, do it heartily, as to the Lord, and not unto men; Knowing that of the Lord ye shall receive the reward of the inheritance: for ye serve the Lord Christ."

We are to be working for the Lord and being obedient to what he would have us do, even when it seems that our work goes unnoticed or is taken for granted. We should never do a sloppy job just because no one will notice or because we don't get the recognition we feel we ought to get when we do a good job. Everything we do should be done as best as we are able and with a good attitude as if we are doing it for Jesus himself.

We also see an interesting passage in Luke 17:7–10:

> But which of you, having a servant plow-
> ing or feeding cattle, will say unto him by and
> by, when he is come from the field, Go and sit

down to meat? And will not rather say unto him, Make ready wherewith I may sup, and gird thyself, and serve me, till I have eaten and drunken; and afterward thou shalt eat and drink? Doth he thank that servant because he did the things that were commanded him? I trow not. So likewise ye, when ye shall have done all those things which are commanded you, say, We are unprofitable servants: we have done that which was our duty to do.

Again, this is not to say we should not thank our children or someone who is working for us, but for each one of us—ourselves—as we are working, we ought to be working with the attitude that we are doing our duty, working as unto the Lord, and no thanks are expected.

When the verse above says, "We are unprofitable servants," the words used there are not intended to indicate that no good or profitable work is done but rather that we have done nothing to put the Lord in debt to us. We have not given him anything that he has not already given to us. He does not owe us anything (including any thanks).

Perhaps you have worked all day in the harsh elements to put bread on the table for your family, and instead of thanks, you only hear that you have not done enough.

Perhaps you worked all day to try to put the house in order, take care of the children, and get supper on the table, and instead of appreciation, you only got irritation.

Perhaps you have cleaned up your toys or helped a sibling or done extra chores without being told, and no one notices and commends you for your help.

Perhaps you have spent time and/or money to try to help a friend, and they seem not to appreciate it or worse yet begin to blame you as part of the problem.

Do we quit, not do a good job, or stop being helpful because our family or friends do not notice, appreciate, or thank us for what we have done? As Christians, we can and are called to do better than this. We are to do all that we do as unto the Lord, not needing the praise of men. We are also to do what we know we ought to do (James 4:17).

And then when we have done all these things, although God owes us nothing at all, our verse above says that "of the Lord ye shall receive the reward." Isn't our God so gracious toward us? Today, let's remember to do everything "heartily, as to the Lord, and not unto men" (Colossians 3:23) and to thank the Lord for the privilege of serving him.

> And whatsoever ye do in word or deed, do all in the name of
> the Lord Jesus, giving thanks to God and the Father by him.
>
> —Colossians 3:17

HOLY
HOLY
HOLY
HOLY
HOLY

Day 6

Have you sat down to pray and quickly said a prayer of thanks before beginning your meal without ever really thinking about to whom you are saying thank you?

Although we know that no man has seen God at any time (John 1:18), the Bible does give a few small glimpses.

In Revelation 4, it says,

> After this I looked, and, behold, a door was opened in heaven: and the first voice...said, Come up hither, and I will shew thee things... behold, a throne was set in heaven, and one sat on the throne. And he that sat was to look upon like a jasper and a sardine stone: and there was a rainbow round about the throne, in sight like unto an emerald. And round about the throne... four and twenty elders sitting, clothed in white raiment; and they had on their heads crowns of gold. And out of the throne proceeded lightnings and thunderings and voices... And before the throne there was a sea of glass like unto crystal: and in the midst of the throne, and round about the throne, were four beasts full of eyes before and behind...and they rest not day and night, saying, Holy, holy, holy, LORD God Almighty, which was, and is, and is to come. And when those beasts give glory and honour and thanks to him that sat on the throne, who liveth for ever and ever. The four and twenty elders fall down before him that

sat on the throne, and worship him that liveth
for ever and ever, and cast their crowns before
the throne, saying, Thou art worthy, O Lord, to
receive glory and honour and power: for thou
hast created all things, and for thy pleasure they
are and were created. (Revelation 4:1–11)

Our God is holy. He is worthy of all glory and honor and thanks.
He is worthy of our full attention. When we pause to thank him as
we go about our day—whether for a meal or some other of all his
blessings—let's remember to whom we are speaking. Let's remember
to not just say thank you, but to do it with the respect and reverence
and sincerity that our great God is so worthy of.

And the four and twenty elders, which sat before God on
their seats, fell upon their faces, and worshipped God,
Saying, We give thee thanks, O Lord God Almighty,
which art, and wast, and art to come; because thou hast
taken to thee thy great power, and hast reigned.

—Revelation 11:16–17

Part 2

Always Thankful

Part 2 Hymn Highlight

Now Thank We All Our God

> Now thank we all our God with heart and hands
> and voices,
> Who wondrous things has done, in whom this
> world rejoices;
> Who, from our mothers' arms has blessed us on
> our way
> With countless gifts of love, and still is ours today.
> O may this bounteous God through all our life
> be near us,
> With ever joyful hearts and blessed peace to cheer
> us;
> And keep us in His grace, and guide us when
> perplexed;
> And free us from all ills, in this world and the
> next!
> All praise and thanks to God the Father now be
> given;
> The Son, and Him who reigns with Them in
> highest Heaven;
> The one eternal God, whom earth and Heaven
> adore;
> For thus it was, is now, and shall be evermore.
> (Martin Rinkart, public domain)

Short Chorus or Children's Song

"Thank You, Lord, for Saving My Soul" (chorus)
by Seth and Bessie Sykes
(Text not printed due to copyright.)

Psalm Highlight

Psalm 136:1–26

> O give thanks unto the LORD; for he is good: for
> his mercy endureth for ever.
> O give thanks unto the God of gods: for his
> mercy endureth for ever.
> O give thanks to the Lord of lords: for his mercy
> endureth for ever.
> To him who alone doeth great wonders: for his
> mercy endureth for ever.
> To him that by wisdom made the heavens: for his
> mercy endureth for ever.
> To him that stretched out the earth above the
> waters: for his mercy endureth for ever.
> To him that made great lights: for his mercy
> endureth for ever:
> The sun to rule by day: for his mercy endureth
> for ever:
> The moon and stars to rule by night: for his
> mercy endureth for ever.
> To him that smote Egypt in their firstborn: for
> his mercy endureth for ever:
> And brought out Israel from among them: for his
> mercy endureth for ever:
> With a strong hand, and with a stretched out
> arm: for his mercy endureth for ever.
> To him which divided the Red sea into parts: for
> his mercy endureth for ever:

And made Israel to pass through the midst of it:
    for his mercy endureth for ever:
But overthrew Pharaoh and his host in the Red
    sea: for his mercy endureth for ever.
To him which led his people through the wilder-
    ness: for his mercy endureth for ever.
To him which smote great kings: for his mercy
    endureth for ever:
And slew famous kings: for his mercy endureth
    for ever:
Sihon king of the Amorites: for his mercy
    endureth for ever:
And Og the king of Bashan: for his mercy
    endureth for ever:
And gave their land for an heritage: for his mercy
    endureth for ever:
Even an heritage unto Israel his servant: for his
    mercy endureth for ever.
Who remembered us in our low estate: for his
    mercy endureth for ever:
And hath redeemed us from our enemies: for his
    mercy endureth for ever.
Who giveth food to all flesh: for his mercy
    endureth for ever.
O give thanks unto the God of heaven: for his
    mercy endureth for ever.

Key Verse

O give thanks unto the Lord; for he is good:
for his mercy endureth for ever. (Psalm 136:1)

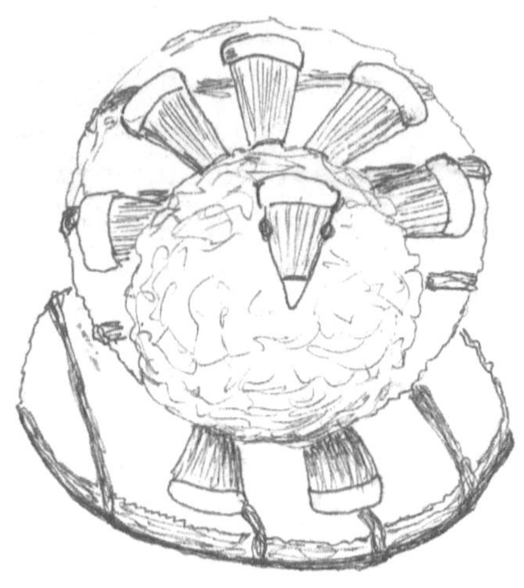

Featured Turkey Recipe
Candy Corn Turkey

You will need the following ingredients:

> Rice Krispies
> Marshmallows

Make into Rice Krispies balls about 2.5-inch diameter.

> 1 package Fudge Stripe cookies
> 1 bag candy corn
> Chocolate or white chocolate (or almond bark)—melted
> 1 tube decorating gel or frosting for eyes

For best results, place Rice Krispies balls and Fudge Stripes cookies in the freezer for fifteen to thirty minutes before you start. Melt the chocolate. Take half of the cookies and use the chocolate to *glue* the candy corn in a half circle around one edge with points facing in. Let it harden. Take the other cookies with no candy and spread some melted chocolate on top. Quickly place a ball on the chocolate. Spread some chocolate on one side of the ball (this will be the back of the turkey) and *glue* one of the cookies with candy corn, facing up onto the side of the ball. Let it harden. Add candy corn for the head and beak and cut pieces for the feet. Use the frosting to make eyes. Great for decorations or gifts, and it's very tasty!

34   EMILY AND DANIEL MYERS

Part 2 Activity
Thankfulness Cards

Years ago, our family received a card from someone we had not seen in a while near Thanksgiving that read, "When I count my blessings, your name keeps coming up," and then went on to write a few lines saying they were thankful for knowing us. I really thought it was nice, and it obviously made a lasting impression. This week's activity is mostly based on that experience.

Go out and collect pretty leaves or just leaves that are not completely dry. Place the leaves between two pieces of wax paper in a large book to press them. This time of year, they should be dry enough to use in a couple days.

While they are drying, make a list—short or long—of some people that you know that you are thankful for or would like to say thank you to for various reasons. Make it short enough that it is still fun and doable.

With adult supervision, use the leaves along with construction paper and/or shaved fall-colored crayons to make some type of card or fall decoration. You can just glue the leaves to the cards or use contact paper to cover them. You can also use laminating pouches, but because it's hard to keep things in place, it sometimes works better to place a piece of fabric over the pouch and use a hot iron to seal them. It also melts the crayon pieces if you use them, adding nice color.

Write a short note or just write "Thank you!"

Of course, you may also use store-bought cards to send your notes.

Mail or hand deliver your creation.

Day 1

More than half of the verses in 1 Thessalonians, five are short state-
ments or thoughts that are two lines long or less. Among these is
verse 18, "In every thing give thanks: for this is the will of God in
Christ Jesus concerning you."

It can be easy to give thanks to God for the good things that
come into our life, but giving thanks for everything is not so easy. It
is only when we truly trust God and believe that he is good like he
says he is that we can really thank God when times are hard. When
we are saved, we can truly be thankful in *every* thing.

Death, disease, loss, sadness—these are not *good* things, so how
can we be thankful for them?

God says in Jeremiah 29:11–13, "For I know the thoughts that
I think toward you, saith the LORD, thoughts of peace, and not of
evil, to give you an expected end. Then shall ye call upon me, and
ye shall go and pray unto me, and I will hearken unto you. And ye
shall seek me, and find me, when ye shall search for me with all your
heart."

In Psalm 91:11, "For he shall give his angels charge over thee, to keep thee in all thy ways."

And probably the most well-known Romans 8:28, "And we know that all things work together for good to them that love God, to them who are the called according to his purpose."

There are many more verses we could add to this list. All through the Bible, we read of God's power, his love, and care. We read that his ways are higher than our ways in Isaiah. We have a sure and steadfast hope. We won't always understand why, but we do know that God knows. He has a plan. He has the power and ability to bring his plan to pass. Because of all these, we truly can thank God in all circumstances—for everything.

> In every thing give thanks: for this is the will of
> God in Christ Jesus concerning you.

—1 Thessalonians 5:18

Day 2

As Joseph said to his brothers in Genesis, "You meant it for evil, but God meant it for good." The story of Squanto is one in which we see what look like tragedies turn out to be the means of saving lives.

Squanto was born in the 1580s near Plymouth, Massachusetts. In 1605, he was kidnapped by Captain George Weymouth and was taken to England as a curiosity to show some of the native people to those back home. Squanto learned some English and was hired as an interpreter and guide. Finally, he returned to his home in 1614 only to be tricked and kidnapped again by an English explorer, Thomas Hunt. He was brought to Spain and sold as a slave. A monk bought Squanto and taught him of Jesus, and from what we can read, it does seem that through that teaching and others who would tell him more over the years, Squanto did trust Jesus and was saved.

Squanto again was able to get back home in 1619, only to find his entire family and Patuxet tribe dead from smallpox. He then lived with a nearby tribe, the Wampanoags, until in 1621, he was introduced to the pilgrims who had settled on the site of his own tribe's village. He found them very unused to how to survive in this new and strange country. He taught them how to plant food and catch game.

Squanto also served as an interpreter and initially helped make peace between the Indians and the pilgrims. He lived with and helped the pilgrims until his death from *Indian fever* in 1622.

Without Squanto, we would likely not have the history of the first Thanksgiving that we have today. This is yet another example of God's providence in guiding the building of our nation on Christian principles.

Who remembered us in our low estate: for his mercy
endureth for ever: And hath redeemed us from our
enemies: for his mercy endureth for ever.

—Psalm 136:23–24

Day 3

The hymn "Now Thank We All Our God" was written during a very difficult time.

The author, Martin Rinkart, was a Lutheran in what is now Germany and became archdeacon of the church at Eilenburg, Saxony, in 1617, just before the start of the Thirty Years' War (from 1618–1648). The city of Eilenburg was a walled city and so became a refuge for many fugitives from far and near. The overcrowding caused famine and disease. The year 1637 was called the year of the Great Pestilence, in which about eight thousand persons died, including Martin Rinkart's wife. At the beginning of the year, there were four pastors in the city. One left to find a safer place; the other two died, leaving only Martin Rinkart. He performed up to forty or fifty funerals a day and personally led burial services for 4,480 people that year

Martin Rinkart never stopped helping the people in his city. He gave away everything he could to help the poor and was barely able to feed and clothe his own children.

Martin Rinkart wanted a song for his children to sing as a prayer before meals, and he wrote "Now Thank We All Our God" during this very difficult time. Later, when the war was finally over, "Now Thank We All Our God" was sung at a national Thanksgiving celebration service.

"Now Thank We All Our God" is Martin Rinkart's best-known hymn, though he wrote over sixty hymns in his lifetime and also wrote seven dramas for the one-hundredth anniversary of the Reformation. His hymn "Now Thank We All Our God" shows how even through such difficulty and sorrow, he was able to trust and thank God, who truly does wondrous things. Martin Rinkart died in December 1649.

Now thank we all our God
With hearts and hands and voices,
Who wondrous things hath done,
In Whom His world rejoices;
Who, from our mothers' arms,
Hath blessed us on our way
With countless gifts of love,
And still is ours today.

O may this bounteous God
Through all our life be near us,
With ever joyful hearts
And blessed peace to cheer us,
And keep us in His grace,
And guide us when perplexed,
And free us from all ills
In this world and the next.

All praise and thanks to God
The Father now be given,
The Son, and Him Who reigns

With them in highest heaven,
The one eternal God,
Whom earth and heav'n adore;
For thus it was, is now,
And shall be evermore.

Unto thee, O God, do we give thanks, unto thee do we give thanks: for that thy name is near thy wondrous works declare.

—Psalm 75:1

Day 4

It was through Paul that God gave us the verse, "In everything give thanks; for this is the will of God in Christ Jesus concerning you," but Paul did not start off thanking God for everything. In fact, he spent all his waking hours hating Christians and doing all he could to get rid of them for some time. Christ personally stopped Paul and spoke to him and blinded him, then sent him to a street called *Straight* (he was sent to the Straight Street—this has always been humorous to me), where the Lord through Ananias restored Paul's sight. The Lord had told Ananias, "I will show him how great things he must suffer for my sake."

Upon being converted, Paul served the Lord with even more zeal than he had persecuted his followers, and for this—as the Lord had shown Ananias—Paul suffered much, but it did not deter him or cause him to grumble. In Acts 16, we read where Paul and Silas—his traveling companion—were thrown into jail for preaching, and at midnight, as they praised the Lord, their chains came off, and the prison doors opened. This resulted in a revival in the house of the jailer.

In 1 Corinthians 11, Paul says, "Be ye followers of me, even as I also am of Christ." Then later on, Paul recalls some troubling afflictions in 2 Corinthians 11:23–28 concerning his trials and saying,

> Are they ministers of Christ? (I speak as a fool) I am more; in labours more abundant, in stripes above measure, in prisons more frequent, in deaths oft. Of the Jews five times received I forty stripes save one. Thrice was I beaten with rods, once was I stoned, thrice I suffered ship-

wreck, a night and a day I have been in the deep;
In journeyings often, in perils of waters, in perils
of robbers, in perils by mine own countrymen, in
perils by the heathen, in perils in the city, in perils in the wilderness, in perils in the sea, in perils
among false brethren; In weariness and painful-
ness, in watchings often, in hunger and thirst,
in fastings often, in cold and nakedness. Beside
those things that are without, that which cometh
upon me daily, the care of all the churches.

What person alive would want to follow Paul's lead? Why should we pattern our lives after Paul? It is because of how, with all that, he served the Lord and how he reacted to all these seemingly bad things that happened to him. Although he did not know why God was allowing him to suffer, he did have faith that God would be glorified in all things. He trusted God fully and presented himself available for his use.

Now thanks be unto God, which always causeth
us to triumph in Christ, and maketh manifest the
savour of his knowledge by us in every place.

—2 Corinthians 2:14

Day 5

Washington, DC
October 3, 1863

By the President of the United States of America.
A Proclamation.

The year that is drawing towards its close, has been filled with the blessings of fruitful fields and healthful skies. To these bounties, which are so constantly enjoyed that we are prone to

forget the source from which they come, others
have been added, which are of so extraordinary
a nature, that they cannot fail to penetrate and
soften even the heart which is habitually insensi-
ble to the ever watchful providence of Almighty
God. In the midst of a civil war of unequalled
magnitude and severity, which has sometimes
seemed to foreign States to invite and to provoke
their aggression, peace has been preserved with
all nations, order has been maintained, the laws
have been respected and obeyed, and harmony
has prevailed everywhere except in the theatre
of military conflict; while that theatre has been
greatly contracted by the advancing armies and
navies of the Union. Needful diversions of wealth
and of strength from the fields of peaceful indus-
try to the national defence, have not arrested
the plough, the shuttle or the ship; the axe has
enlarged the borders of our settlements, and the
mines, as well of iron and coal as of the precious
metals, have yielded even more abundantly than
heretofore. Population has steadily increased,
notwithstanding the waste that has been made
in the camp, the siege and the battle-field; and
the country, rejoicing in the consciousness of
augmented strength and vigor, is permitted to
expect continuance of years with large increase
of freedom. No human counsel hath devised
nor hath any mortal hand worked out these
great things. They are the gracious gifts of the
Most High God, who, while dealing with us in
anger for our sins, hath nevertheless remembered
mercy. It has seemed to me fit and proper that
they should be solemnly, reverently and grate-
fully acknowledged as with one heart and one
voice by the whole American People. I do there-

fore invite my fellow citizens in every part of the United States, and also those who are at sea and those who are sojourning in foreign lands, to set apart and observe the last Thursday of November next, as a day of Thanksgiving and Praise to our beneficent Father who dwelleth in the Heavens. And I recommend to them that while offering up the ascriptions justly due to Him for such singular deliverances and blessings, they do also, with humble penitence for our national perverseness and disobedience, commend to His tender care all those who have become widows, orphans, mourners or sufferers in the lamentable civil strife in which we are unavoidably engaged, and fervently implore the interposition of the Almighty Hand to heal the wounds of the nation and to restore it as soon as may be consistent with the Divine purposes to the full enjoyment of peace, harmony, tranquillity and Union.

In testimony whereof, I have hereunto set my hand and caused the Seal of the United States to be affixed.

Done at the City of Washington, this Third day of October, in the year of our Lord one thousand eight hundred and sixty-three, and of the Independence of the United States the Eighty-eighth.

By the President: Abraham Lincoln.
(Abraham Lincoln's Thanksgiving
Proclamation in 1863)

Being enriched in every thing to all bountifulness, which causeth through us thanksgiving to God.

—2 Corinthians 9:12

Day 6

Most of us offer a prayer of thanks at every meal we eat while sitting in our houses or perhaps in our car or at a nice outdoor picnic site. Very often, we offer our thanks in our churches, but where is the most difficult place you have physically been and thanked God?

In places of distress, we cry out to God for help, and often, when God brings us into a better place, we rightly give thanks. How often though, after asking God's help, do we, knowing that God hears us and knows best, begin to thank God in faith when we are still in our hard place and can't see how God will help us yet?

In the story of Jonah, after disobeying God and running into a storm and then being thrown into the sea and swallowed by a great fish, Jonah prays to God.

He ends his prayer inside the fish with "But I will sacrifice unto thee with the voice of thanksgiving; I will pay that that I have vowed. Salvation is of the Lord" (Jonah 2:9). In the very next verse, Jonah is delivered—"And the Lord spake unto the fish, and it vomited out Jonah upon the dry land" (Jonah 2:10).

Next time you are in a hard place, don't just ask the Lord for help, but come to him with thanksgiving for who he is and what he has and will do.

> I will offer to thee the sacrifice of thanksgiving,
> and will call upon the name of the Lord.
>
> —Psalm 116:17

Part 3

Sincere Thankfulness

Part 3 Hymn Highlight

We Plow the Fields and Scatter the Good Seed on the Land

1. We plow the fields and scatter
    The good seed on the land,
    But it is fed and watered
    By God's almighty hand:
    He sends the snow in winter,
    The warmth to swell the grain,
    The breezes, and the sunshine,
    And soft, refreshing rain.

    Refrain:
    All good gifts around us
    Are sent from heav'n above;
    Then thank the Lord, oh, thank the Lord,
    For all His love.

2. He only is the Maker
    Of all things near and far;
    He paints the wayside flower,
    He lights the evening star;
    The winds and waves obey Him,
    By Him the birds are fed;
    Much more to us, His children,
    He gives our daily bread.

3. We thank Thee then, O Father,
    For all things bright and good,

The seedtime and the harvest,
Our life, our health, our food;
Accept the gifts we offer
For all Thy love imparts,
And what Thou most desirest—
Our humble, thankful hearts.
(Matthias Claudius)

Short Chorus or Children's Song

If You're Thankful

If You're Thankful and you know it clap your
hands (clap, clap)
If You're Thankful and you know it clap your
hands
If You're Thankful and you know it then your life
will surely show it.
If You're Thankful and you know it clap your
hands

If You're Thankful and you know it praise Him
now!
(Praise God—lift hands)
If You're Thankful and you know it praise Him
now!
(Praise God—lift hands)
If You're Thankful and you know it then your life
will surely show it.
If You're Thankful and you know it praise Him
now!
(Praise God—lift hands) (Author Unknown,
public domain)

Psalm Highlight

Psalm 147:1–11

Praise ye the LORD: for it is good to sing praises
unto our God; for it is pleasant; and praise
is comely.
The LORD doth build up Jerusalem: he gathereth
together the outcasts of Israel.
He healeth the broken in heart, and bindeth up
their wounds.
He telleth the number of the stars; he calleth
them all by their names.
Great is our Lord, and of great power: his understanding is infinite.
The LORD lifteth up the meek: he casteth the
wicked down to the ground.
Sing unto the LORD with thanksgiving; sing
praise upon the harp unto our God:
Who covereth the heaven with clouds, who pre-
pareth rain for the earth, who maketh grass
to grow upon the mountains.
He giveth to the beast his food, and to the young
ravens which cry.
He delighteth not in the strength of the horse:
he taketh not pleasure in the legs of a man.
The LORD taketh pleasure in them that fear him,
in those that hope in his mercy.

Key Verse

Sing unto the LORD with thanksgiving; sing
praise upon the harp unto our God. (Psalm 147:7)

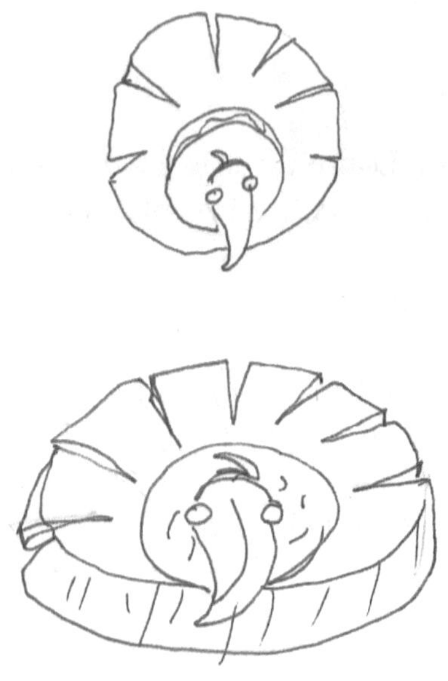

Featured Turkey Recipe
Potatoes and Peppers (Side)

You will need the following ingredients:

> One or more large (big around) sweet potato
> Several small white (red or russet) potatoes
> A few red/orange/yellow sweet peppers
> Toothpicks
> Mustard (optional)

Using the picture as a guide. Slice the sweet potato into 1/2–3/4 thick rounds. Slice the white potatoes a bit thinner.

Line a baking pan with parchment paper (optional: spray with cooking spray).

Arrange sweet potato rounds on paper. Place a small white potato round on top. Cut a sweet pepper for the head and beak and use a toothpick to attach it to the white potato. When all are ready, brush or spray with oil (optional) and bake at 400 degrees Fahrenheit until soft (about thirty minutes?).

With a knife, cut out a triangle of sweet potato on each side, then cut the top into feathers and gently separate just a little to get a more feathery look. Alternately just score the top—faster.

Use mustard if desired to make eyes. Serve with your favorite meat!

60   EMILY AND DANIEL MYERS

Part 3 Activity
Rocking Pilgrim Egg Men

Adult supervision is needed!

The materials you will need:

> Raw eggs
> Wax—can use melted crayons
> Black construction paper
> Black Sharpie
> Wite-Out liquid
> School glue stick
> Optional: For more elaborate pilgrims, use felt or
> fabric scraps and fabric or hot glue.

With the point of a paring knife, gently make a small hole in the top of each egg. Using a toothpick or skewer, dump egg contents into a bowl to use in a recipe later (omelets for breakfast?). Preferably, let the eggshells dry for a day.

In an old tin can or disposable aluminum pan or something you don't care about, melt the wax or crayons. Be *very* careful with hot wax.

Make sure the eggs are sitting up very straight in an egg carton and then carefully pour the wax into the bottom of each—only fill about 1/2 inch in the bottom. Do not touch or move the eggs until they're cool.

When the eggs are cool, they will always stand upright (if the wax is even) and will rock and stay up when pushed.

Use the construction paper to make little hats to glue over the holes. Use the marker and Wite-Out for face and clothes. Be creative and make a whole family.

Day 1

In that hour, Jesus rejoiced in spirit and said, "I thank thee, O Father, Lord of heaven and earth, that thou hast hid these things from the wise and prudent, and hast revealed them unto babes: even so, Father; for so it seemed good in thy sight. All things are delivered to me of my Father: and no man knoweth who the Son is, but the Father; and who the Father is, but the Son, and he to whom the Son will reveal him" (Luke 10:21–22).

Jesus set the example for us in all things while on earth. Jesus was God in the flesh, but he spent much time in prayer. Jesus gave thanks to God as an example for us to follow.

When Jesus fed the five thousand, and when he fed the four thousand, we are told he first gave thanks and then gave the bread and fish to the disciple to feed the people. Yes, Jesus had the power to multiply the food, but we can follow his example as we are obedient in doing what he has for us to do. God is able in many ways to *multiply the loaves and fish.*

One example of this is that of George Muller when he had so many orphans and no food to feed them. He had them sit down as usual to eat. He prayed, thanking God and asking that their need be supplied, and they were supplied with both bread and milk for breakfast by the time he had done praying.

When Jesus raised Lazarus from the dead, he prayed and said, "Father, I thank thee that thou hast heard me. And I knew that thou hearest me always: but because of the people which stand by I said it, that they may believe that thou hast sent me" (John 11:41–42). In this place, he specifically lets us know that he is giving thanks to God as an example to us.

Again, at the last supper, we read that Jesus took the bread and the cup—what would become the symbols of his suffering and death on the cross to pay the price for our sins—and he gave thanks.

Jesus gave thanks. Let's remember to thank him today.

At that time Jesus answered and said, I thank thee, O Father, Lord of heaven and earth, because thou hast hid these things from the wise and prudent, and hast revealed them unto babes.

—Matthew 11:25

Day 2

The kindly old king was awake with the dawn! "Today is the day!" said the king with a yawn. He jumped out of bed, put the crown on his head, and dressed himself quickly in robes of bright red. As a child, I liked books that rhymed, and I still do. This one I can still recite almost all by heart (although there are just a couple lines I can't recall). This book was not just a good rhyme, though, but it's a good story based on Jesus's parable of the unforgiving servant.

Usually, when we read it, we are thinking about forgiveness as that is the parable's main message. However, we see that this servant was also given a very great gift, forgiveness of a huge debt, but he was not thankful—or at least not truly thankful.

In the story book referenced above, on hearing that his debt is forgiven, the book continues, "Oh thank you, my king," cried the servant with glee. "I'll always remember your kindness to me." Now we know that this is only a storybook and the Bible does not specifically say whether the servant thanked the king, but his actions showed that he was not truly thankful.

How often do we say thank you, either to God or to others, and then show through our actions that we are not truly thankful? We bow our heads at mealtime but then complain about the food or about the dishes afterward. We say thank you for a new toy or gift and then leave it out where it is broken or destroyed. When we do things such as this, are we really thankful in the true definition of the word?

In James 3, it says,

> Out of the same mouth proceedeth blessing and cursing. My brethren, these things ought not so to be. Doth a fountain send forth at the same place sweet water and bitter? Can the fig tree, my brethren, bear olive berries? either a vine, figs? so can no fountain both yield salt water and fresh. (James 3:10–12)

When we are truly thankful, it will change our behavior. We cannot be truly thankful and grumble at the same time. If we truly begin to understand how much God has done for us, our thankfulness to God will change how we treat our fellow man.

As ye have therefore received Christ Jesus the Lord, so walk ye
in him: Rooted and built up in him, and stablished in the faith,
as ye have been taught, abounding therein with thanksgiving.

—Colossians 2:6–7

Morning Routine

Day 3

In this Thanksgiving proclamation given by Theodore Roosevelt on October 31, 1908, he recommended that the day of thanksgiving be set aside so that "people shall cease from their daily work, and in their homes or in their churches, meet devoutly to thank the Almighty." No mention of feasting is made here.

His proclamation was in part as follows:

> Once again, the season is at hand when, according to the ancient custom of our people, it becomes the duty of the President to appoint a day of prayer and of thanksgiving to God.
>
> Year by year this Nation grows…we have grown and prospered in material things to a degree never known before, and not now known in any other country. The thirteen colonies which straggled along the seacoast of the Atlantic and were hemmed-in but a few miles west of tidewater by the Indian haunted wilderness, have been transformed into the mightiest republic which the world has ever seen… For the very reason that in material well-being we have thus abounded, we owe it to the Almighty to show equal progress in moral and spiritual things… The things of the body are good; the things of the intellect better; the best of all are the things of the soul; for, in the nation as in the individual, in the long run it is character that counts. Let us, therefore, as a people set our faces resolutely against evil, and

with broad charity, with kindliness and good-will toward all men, but with unflinching determination to smite down wrong, strive with all the strength that is given us for righteousness in public and in private life.

Now, Therefore, I, Theodore Roosevelt, President of the United States, do set apart Thursday, the 26th day of November, next, as a day of general thanksgiving and prayer, and on that day I recommend that the people shall cease from their daily work, and, in their homes or in their churches, meet devoutly to thank the Almighty for the many and great blessings they have received in the past, and to pray that they may be given the strength so to order their lives as to deserve a continuation of these blessings in the future. (Theodore Roosevelt's Proclamation 822—Thanksgiving Day, 1908)

I exhort therefore, that, first of all, supplications, prayers,
intercessions, and giving of thanks, be made for all men;
For kings, and for all that are in authority; that we may lead
a quiet and peaceable life in all godliness and honesty.

—1 Timothy 2:1–2

Day 4

We have been learning how important it is to thank the Lord for all he has done in all circumstances and all the time. Today, we will look at another reason to thank the Lord. In Psalm 92:1, it simply states that "it is a good thing."

We should thank our God simply because it is good to thank him!

As we looked at before, to give thanks to God is to show appreciation, to show gratitude, to acknowledge indebtedness, to bless, to acknowledge our sinful state before a holy God, and to do this with joy!

So it is a good thing to express to God that we appreciate who he is and what he has done.

It is a good thing to be grateful for all God has done, both in word and in deed, by taking care of what he has given us or extending to others the same graces that he bestows on us.

It is a good thing to acknowledge how utterly lost and sinful we were without him and would still be, but for his great love wherewith he loved us.

It is a good thing to rejoice before the Lord by singing his praises, by celebrating with feasting on those things he has so richly blessed us with, and by sharing this joy and bounty with friends.

> It is a good thing to give thanks unto the Lord, and
> to sing praises unto thy name, O Most High.

> —Psalm 92:1

Day 5

In the parable of the ten lepers, we see just how easy it is to receive a blessing from God without being thankful and responding in gratefulness to this blessing.

Ten lepers called to Jesus for healing.

Ten lepers needed healing for their terrible condition.

Ten men called out to Jesus to have mercy on them.

Interestingly, Jesus did not immediately just heal them but told them to go show themselves to the priest, as the law prescribed, to be pronounced clean. It appears that all ten of the lepers must have had some faith as they all started off to the priest, and as they went—in obedience to Jesus's instructions—they were healed.

And so ten lepers received healing from Jesus—ten, yet only one turned and went to Jesus and thanked him for this wonderful, powerful thing Jesus had done for him. We are told that as he was going, when he saw that he was healed, he "turned back, and with a loud voice glorified God, And fell down on *his* face at his feet, giving him [Jesus] thanks" (Luke 17:15b–16a).

Jesus's answer was to ask: "Were there not ten cleansed? But where are the nine?"

The nine lepers seemed to show a heart of ingratitude and thanklessness. They did not seem to even realize the great gift they had been given. Their hearts appeared cold toward God, indifferent to his act of love and mercy.

We look at those nine and wonder; we think we would be like the one who returned to give thanks, but how often do we forget just how dependent we are on God for our every breath. Let us learn from the thankful healed leper and, even when those around us do not, take time to see, appreciate, and thank God for the daily blessings he bestows on us.

> That I may publish with the voice of thanksgiving,
> and tell of all thy wondrous works.

> —Psalm 26:7

MÊ NÊ   MÊ NÊ
TÊ KÊL U

Day 6

Each day, we are being watched and weighed for how we obey and love God. We are responsible for what we know. We are responsible for all the things that we have been shown and learned from God in our past. Our witness to those around us is to glorify God and honor him.

There once was a great king. In fact, he was the greatest king in the world. One day, he was walking through his castle and thinking—no, not just thinking but boasting aloud of how great his kingdom had become. And while he was saying that he was the reason for his greatness, God ripped his kingdom, his pride, and even human likeness from him. God cast him out of his palace, and he was made to live like an animal until the king remembered *who* it was that gave him all he had. After a long time, the king did look up and repented for his pride, giving God all the glory due for his blessings.

And so it was that years later the king's son, Belshazzar, held a great feast in his honor. Belshazzar wanted to show just how great he had become. He had the finest dishes used for the feast, including the golden, silver, and brass vessels from the house of the Lord. Belshazzar was praised. All the gods of gold, silver, and man-made things were praised. Suddenly, a man's hand appeared and wrote the truth on the wall. Belshazzar was shocked and frightened. Daniel was called to interpret the writing.

He reminded the king of all that had happened to his father and continued,

> And thou his son, O Belshazzar, hast not
> humbled thine heart, though thou knewest all
> this; But hast lifted up thyself against the Lord

of heaven; and they have brought the vessels of
his house before thee, and thou, and thy lords,
thy wives, and thy concubines, have drunk wine
in them; and thou hast praised the gods of silver, and gold, of brass, iron, wood, and stone,
which see not, nor hear, nor know: and the God
in whose hand thy breath is, and whose are all thy
ways, hast thou not glorified. (Daniel 5:22–23)

He was told that he had been weighed and found wanting. His
kingdom would be ripped from him and divided up for his enemies
to rule.

He had forgotten about his father and the events that led his
father back to praising and honoring God. He already knew what
was right but decided not to do it.

Offer unto God thanksgiving; and pay
thy vows unto the most High.

—Psalm 50:14

Part 4

Thanksgiving Then and Now

Part 4 Hymn Highlight

We Gather Together

> We gather together to ask the Lord's blessing;
> He chastens and hastens his will to make known;
> The wicked oppressing now cease from distressing:
> Sing praises to his name; he forgets not his own.
> Beside us to guide us, our God with us joining,
> Whose kingdom calls all to the love which endures.
> So from the beginning the fight we were winning:
> You, Lord, were at our side; all glory be yours!
> We all do extol you, our leader triumphant,
> And pray that you still our defender will be.
> Let your congregation escape tribulation:
> Your name be ever praised! O Lord, make us free!
> (Anonymous (1625), trans. Theodore Baker)

Short Chorus or Children's Song

Thanksgiving Day Is a Happy Day

> Thanksgiving Day is a happy day and we say
>   Thank you God
> Thanksgiving Day is a happy day and we say
>   Thank you God
> Thanksgiving Day is a happy day and we go to
>   Grandma's house
> Thanksgiving Day is a happy day and we go to
>   Grandma's house

Thanksgiving Day is a happy day and we eat
    pumpkin pie
Thanksgiving Day is a happy day and we eat
    pumpkin pie

Psalm Highlight

Psalm 100

Make a joyful noise unto the LORD, all ye lands.

Serve the LORD with gladness: come before his presence with singing.

Know ye that the LORD is God: it is he that hath made us, and not we ourselves; we are his people, and the sheep of his pasture.

Enter into his gates with thanksgiving, and into his courts with praise: be thankful unto him, and bless his name.

For the LORD is good; his mercy is everlasting; and his truth endureth to all generations.

Key Verse

I will praise the name of God with a song, and will magnify him with thanksgiving. (Psalm 69:30)

Featured Turkey Recipe
Festive Pumpkin Protein Pancakes with Fruit

For pancakes, you will need (feel free to substitute with your favorite pancake recipe):

  1 cup oats
  2 eggs
  1/2 cup cottage cheese or soft goat cheese
  1/4 cup puree pumpkin
  1 tablespoon maple syrup
  1 tablespoon pumpkin pie spice
  1/2 teaspoon cinnamon
  2 teaspoons baking powder
  1/2 teaspoon salt

Also needed:

Banana(s), mandarin oranges, raisins, and honey or maple syrup to drizzle on top (optional)

Add all the pancake ingredients to the blender and process until smooth. Add a few tablespoons of milk or flour if needed to make a good consistency.

Make slightly small pancakes. Using the sketch as a guide, arrange the fruit on the pancakes—banana for the head, the orange sections for the feathers and beak, and raisins for the eyes and feet, then drizzle with honey just before serving. Gobble, gobble!

Part 4 Activity
Pilgrim Trivia Game

Use the following questions and answers. Make cards to set on the table at Thanksgiving dinner. Cards can be plain or decorated as you like. Answers can be on paper for one designated person or written on the back of each card.

1. How many passengers set sail from England on board the *Mayflower*, and how many arrived?

    One hundred two passengers sailed over on the *Mayflower*, and one hundred two arrived.
    One passenger, Deacon Samuel Fuller's servant named William Butten, died at sea, and one infant was born.

2. Who was the child born on the *Mayflower* during the crossing?

    Oceanus, son of Stephen and Elizabeth Hopkins.

3. How many days did it take the *Mayflower* to cross the Atlantic?

    The *Mayflower*'s crossing took sixty-six days.

4.   Who was the first pilgrim child born after the ship arrived?

Peregrine White, son of William and Susanna White.

5.   When did the pilgrims first set foot on American soil?

On November 11, 1620, in present-day Provincetown, Massachusetts, at the tip of Cape Cod.

6.   How many men made up the pilgrims' first exploring party?

Sixteen well-armed men landed first and explored.

7.   Who was Plymouth Colony's first governor?

John Carver was elected twice: once in November of 1620 aboard the *Mayflower* and again in March of 1621. He died in April of 1621.

8.   Who were the first pilgrims to be married in New England?

Edward Winslow and Susanna White—both widowed during the first winter. They were married in a civil ceremony, as was the custom, on May 12, 1621.

9.   How many pilgrim women survived until the first Thanksgiving feast?

Only four of the married women survived: Elizabeth Hopkins, Eleanor Billington, Susanna White Winslow, and Mary Brewster. These four women, along with the older girls, oversaw food preparation for the three-day harvest feast for the colonists, Massasoit and his ninety Indian men—the feast that we now call "the first Thanksgiving."

10. What eating utensil would not have been found at the harvest feast of 1621?

The pilgrims didn't use forks. They used a knife, a spoon, a large napkin, and their fingers, and shared plates and drinking vessels.

11. What was the name of the Indian that helped the pilgrims learn to plant and survive?

Squanto.

12. What is the title of William Bradford's history of the early years of the colony?

The book is titled *Of Plimoth Plantation.* It was written by the second governor in his later years.

Day 1

Have you been to a parade, game, or gathering where there are crowds of people who are excited and cheering? Think of the biggest, most excited crowd you have been a part of. Now imagine you are there—just ahead is a big crowd of people who are rejoicing, shouting, playing instruments, and dancing. As you come up to the glad and joyous gathering, you notice they are all moving slowly up the road toward Jerusalem. Psalteries, harps, cymbals, and coronets sound out the glad music. You push further through the crowd.

Now you can make out the words of the song of praise:

> Give thanks unto the Lord, call upon his name, make known his deeds among the people. Sing unto him, sing psalms unto him, talk ye of all his wondrous works. Glory ye in his holy name: let the heart of them rejoice that seek the Lord. Seek the Lord and his strength, seek his face continually. Remember his marvelous works that he hath done, his wonders, and the judgments of his mouth.

You press through a little further and break through most of the crowd. Just ahead, several priests are walking, holding between them on poles a box-like structure. A man in a white linen robe and wearing an ephod is going before the procession, dancing and playing on a harp. It's the ark of the covenant of the Lord, and that man is King David!

All around the music continues:

> Sing unto the Lord, all the earth; shew forth
> from day to day his salvation. Declare his glory
> among the heathen; his marvelous works among
> all nations. For great is the Lord, and greatly to
> be praised: he also is to be feared above all gods.
> For all the gods of the people are idols: but the
> Lord made the heavens. Glory and honour are
> in his presence; strength and gladness are in his
> place. Give unto the Lord, ye kindred of the peo-
> ple, give unto the Lord glory and strength. Give
> unto the Lord the glory due unto his name: bring
> an offering, and come before him: worship the
> Lord in the beauty of holiness. Fear before him,
> all the earth: the world also shall be stable, that
> it be not moved. Let the heavens be glad, and
> let the earth rejoice: and let men say among the
> nations, The Lord reigneth. Let the sea roar, and
> the fullness thereof: let the fields rejoice, and all
> that is therein. Then shall the trees of the wood
> sing out at the presence of the Lord, because he
> cometh to judge the earth. O give thanks unto
> the Lord; for he is good; for his mercy endureth
> for ever.

You are swept along with the happy crowd. Now they are just
approaching Jerusalem, and the tent is prepared and ready for the
ark. The priests, though they will surely be glad to rest, don't seem as
tired as if they had just walked six miles. They have been obedient to
God's commands, and he has helped them!

Now it sounds as if their song is coming to an end. Listen.

> And say ye, Save us, O God of our salva-
> tion, and gather us together, and deliver us from
> the heathen, that we may give thanks to thy holy

name, and glory in thy praise. Blessed be the
Lord God of Israel for ever and ever.

As the song ends, all around the air is filled with the sounds of all the people joining in *amen* and praising the Lord.

Now the priests are offering peace offerings and thanksgiving offerings, and what's that over there? As you draw closer, you see that King David is directing that each person "be given a loaf of bread and a good piece of flesh and a flagon of wine" as part of the celebration feast!

Everyone is so happy and joyful. Just then, you glance up at the nearby palace: a very nice place indeed. Suddenly, your eyes catch some movement, and you look again. Yes, there in the window, a woman is looking out, but unlike the rest of the happy crowd, her face shows only disgust—a feeling like a cold wind runs through you as the woman disappears back away from the window. You turn back toward the crowd; they did not notice her, and they continue their praise! The ark of God has come home to them! They are rejoicing in God's goodness, and the disgust of the woman goes unnoticed. Far from dampening their rejoicing, it only hurts the one who chooses to despise instead of joining in praising God (adapted from 1 Chronicles 15 and 16).

There will always be those in our lives who will mock us for praising and thanking God, but our duty is to praise and thank him anyway. Our Lord is worthy and has himself borne shame for us in dying for our sins.

> Give thanks unto the Lord, call upon his name,
> make known his deeds among the people.
>
> —1 Chronicles 16:8

Day 2

Pilgrims: A pilgrim is a person who goes on
a long journey, often to a foreign country, usually
with a religious purpose.

The people we now refer to as *pilgrims* were first called separatists in the early 1600s. The separatists believed much like the puritans, though not as exclusive, and whereas the puritans believed that it was possible to change the Church of England from within, the separatists believed that they must leave—separate from the church. William Bradford wrote of their decision to sail to America: "They knew they were pilgrims, and looked not much on those things, but lifted up their eyes to the heavens, their dearest country; and quieted their spirits."

Another interesting fact is the first baby born after the *Mayflower* arrived in America (a boy born to William and Susannah White) was named Peregrine—a word which means "traveling from far away" and also means "pilgrim." He lived until his eighties, though his father died that first winter.

These people were referred to more and more often as *pilgrims*, and by the early 1800s, it was the popular term used for all the *Mayflower* passengers and also for the others that arrived in Plymouth in those early years, even though not all were separatists. So the English people who settled in Plymouth in the 1620s are most often called the pilgrims, and for simplicity, we will refer to them here as pilgrims.

Most of the pilgrims had left England in 1607–08 because it was illegal to be part of any church other than the Church of England. They settled in Leiden, Holland, and had—for the most part—religious freedom. They remained there for about twelve years. Their main reason for leaving to try to settle in America was the bad influence of the surrounding society on their young people. There was also fear of another war beginning.

The pilgrims had planned to settle near the Jamestown, Virginia, colony. They did not have enough money and so got some investors to help pay for their passage, and they, in turn, would work for the investors for the first seven years, sending back timber, furs, etc. The whole congregation was not able to sail at one time, and most of them, including their pastor—John Robinson—stayed in Holland, hoping to join them later.

The pilgrims ended up with a much later start than they anticipated at first, having to turn back twice due to leaks in one of their ships—the *Speedwell*. Finally, on September 6, 1620, the *Mayflower* alone left England with 102 passengers. Several who had intended to go at first had to stay behind. Only about half of the passengers were actually separatists. Among the passengers, there were about thirty children on board, including a few orphans. One baby was born during the voyage.

After a voyage of sixty-six days, the *Mayflower* arrived in New England on November 11, 1620. To preserve order, before going ashore, all the men (excluding the crew) on the ship signed the document that we know as the *Mayflower* Compact. It laid the foundation for the community's government. The *Mayflower* Compact was a fairly short document.

It reads in part:

> In the name of God, Amen. We, whose names are underwritten,… Having undertaken for the Glory of God, and Advancement of the Christian Faith, and the Honour of our King and Country, a voyage to plant the first colony in the northern parts of Virginia; do by these presents, solemnly and mutually in the Presence of God and one of another, covenant and combine ourselves together into a civil Body Politick,

for our better Ordering and Preservation, and Furtherance of the Ends aforesaid;

And by Virtue hereof to enact, constitute, and frame, such just and equal Laws, Ordinances, Acts, Constitutions and Offices, from time to time, as shall be thought most meet and convenient for the General good of the Colony. (The text of the *Mayflower* Compact)

And out of them shall proceed thanksgiving and the voice of them that make merry: and I will multiply them, and they shall not be few; I will also glorify them, and they shall not be small.

—Jeremiah 30:19

96   EMILY AND DANIEL MYERS

Day 3

(Continued from day 2.) The pilgrims were worried about danger from the Indians when they first arrived, so they sent sixteen well-armed men to land and explore. Looking for a natural harbor for the ship and a good site to settle, they traveled up the coast. They experienced a couple not-so-friendly encounters with Indians and found a few baskets of corn and beans, some of which they took back to the ship, intending to pay the Indians for it when they were able to meet them (which they did about six months after). Bradford writes that they likely would all have died had it not been for finding these provisions. They were disappointed in not finding a suitable place to settle.

Again, on December 6, a party of ten men set out, traveling up the coast in a small boat. It was very cold, and they again met with some hostile Indians, and the stormy weather almost caused them to lose their boat. When the storm was over, they found a harbor that seemed deep enough for the ship, and upon exploring the shore, they found what looked like several abandoned cornfields and little running brooks with plenty of fresh water.

The *Mayflower* arrived in Plymouth harbor on December 16, 1620, and the men went ashore and began to build, beginning with a large house for common use. While houses were being built, the women and children remained on the ship. Only one person had died during the voyage, but now many people began to fall ill. Approximately half of the pilgrims died that first winter in Plymouth. Half of the crew of the *Mayflower* also died before it left for England on April 5, 1621. Despite all their hardships, when they were given the option to return on the *Mayflower* by the kind Captain Jones, all the pilgrims chose to stay.

The pilgrims had no direct contact with the Indians in that first winter, seeing them only from afar. But in the middle of March 1621, an Indian came boldly into their settlement and spoke to them in broken English! They were surprised. The Indian's name was Samoset. Later, he brought another Indian, Squanto, who knew fluent English and taught the pilgrims how to grow food and catch fish and game in this wild new country. Without the help of Squanto, the pilgrims most likely would not have survived. Samoset and Squanto also helped the pilgrims to make peace with the neighboring Indian tribe, which lasted for twenty-four years.

With Squanto's help, the pilgrims had quite a good harvest in the fall and thanked God for this bountiful harvest that promised to make this winter easier than the last.

Although we speak of the pilgrims' first *Thanksgiving* in 1621 with the Indians as if it were a very big event, it is interesting to note that Governor William Bradford hardly mentions it in his book, *History of Plymouth Plantation*, which is the main source of written history of that time. There is one other eyewitness account by Edward Winslow, which also does not give many details, and so much of what we hear about that first thanksgiving is from stories passed down through the generations with no real basis of whether they are truly accurate.

This first Thanksgiving lasted for three days and took place somewhere between the end of September and the beginning of November in 1621. We do have a record that it was attended by the remaining pilgrims: only four of the married women had survived, twenty-two men, and twenty-seven children. It was also attended by the Indian chief, Massasoit, with ninety of his warriors. There is also no record of exactly what was served at this feast, but Bradford writes of an abundance of fish, wild fowl, turkeys, venison, and Indian corn.

Although they had suffered so much, the Lord had protected and provided for them, and now they gave thanks. This was by no means the end of their troubles, as the arrival of thirty-five more pilgrims, along with no supplies, in November made the harvest they expected to be plenty to have need of being stretched much more. Indeed, before their harvest in both 1622 and 23, supplies were so low that it is said that each was allotted just a few kernels of corn each day, along with whatever fish, clams, groundnuts, and deer or fowl could be hunted.

The harvest of 1623 was very good, and never again did the pilgrims face hunger and starvation.

> May not and ought not the children of these fathers rightly say: Our fathers were Englishmen which came over this great ocean, and were ready to perish in this wilderness but they cried unto the Lord, and He heard their voice, and looked on their adversity, &c. Let them therefore praise the Lord, because He is good, and His mercies endure forever. Yea, let them which have been redeemed of the Lord, shew how He hath delivered them from the hand of the oppressor. When they wandered in the; desert wilderness out of the way, and found no city to dwell in, both hungry, and thirsty, their soul was overwhelmed in them. Let them confess before the Lord His loving kindness, and His wonderful works before the sons of men. (William Bradford, *History of Plymouth Plantation*)

Therefore I will give thanks unto thee, O Lord, among the heathen, and I will sing praises unto thy name.

—2 Samuel 22:50

Day 4

Once upon a time, or to be more exact, when time first began, it was then that God made man. God created that first man and woman perfectly; there was no sin. They lived in a beautiful garden and were given the easy task of tending it. They walked with God in this beautiful garden. They had all they needed. There was just one rule: do not eat from the tree in the midst of the garden—the tree of the knowledge of good and evil.

Everything was perfect until they disobeyed. Satan tempted Eve, and instead of believing God, she ate the fruit and gave some to Adam, who also ate it. They did not get the wonderful things the serpent had told them they would get, but they did get separation from God, sin, sorrow, and death!

> By one man sin entered into the world, and
> death by sin; and so death passed upon all men,
> for that all have sinned. (Romans 5:12)

The story is one that is well-known, but an important one to understand why Jesus had to come, why he had to suffer and die. God is holy; nothing sinful can be in his presence. Because of sin, we are separated from God with no way to be reconciled to him. God could have left us all to die in our sins.

> But God, who is rich in mercy, for his great
> love wherewith he loved us, Even when we were
> dead in sins, hath quickened us together with
> Christ, (by grace ye are saved;). (Ephesians 2:4–5)

God sent his Son, Jesus, to be born, live a sinless life among us, and then die to pay the debt for our sins and rise again from the dead. He not only paid for our sins, but he broke the power of death "that whosoever believeth in him should not perish, but have everlasting life" (John 3:16).

Of all God's wonderful gifts that we ought to thank him for, surely this—the gift of his Son Jesus—is the most wonderful of all, and indeed the one that makes all the others so good also.

Thanks be unto God for his unspeakable gift.

—2 Corinthians 9:15

QUILLS
INK

Day 5

And now a very recent Thanksgiving proclamation that rehearses much of the history we have already reviewed:

> On Thanksgiving Day, we remember with reverence and gratitude the bountiful blessings afforded to us by our Creator, and we recommit to sharing in a spirit of thanksgiving and generosity with our friends, neighbors, and families.
>
> Nearly four centuries ago, determined individuals with a vision of a more prosperous life and an abundance of made a pilgrimage to a distant land. These Pilgrims embarked on their journey across the Atlantic at great personal risk, facing unforeseen trials and tribulations, and unforetold hardships during their passage. After their arrival in the New World, a harsh and deadly winter took the lives of half their population. Those who survived remained unwavering in their faith and foresight of a future rich with liberty and freedom, enduring every impediment as they established one of our Nation's first settlements. Through God's divine providence, a meaningful relationship was forged with the Wampanoag Tribe, and through their unwavering resolve and resilience, the Pilgrims enjoyed a bountiful harvest the following year. The celebration of this harvest lasted 3 days and saw Pilgrims and Wampanoag seated together at the table of friendship and unity. That

first Thanksgiving provided an enduring symbol of gratitude that is uniquely sewn into the fabric of our American spirit.

More than 150 years later, it was in this same spirit of unity that President George Washington declared a National Day of Thanksgiving following the Revolutionary War and the ratification of our Constitution. Less than a century later, that hard-won unity came under duress as the United States was engaged in a civil war that threatened the very existence of our Republic. the Battle of Gettysburg in 1863, in an effort to unite the country and acknowledge "the gracious gifts of the Most High God," President Abraham Lincoln asked the American people to come together and "set apart and observe the last Thursday of November next as a Day of Thanksgiving and Praise to our beneficent Father who dwelleth in the heavens." Today, this tradition continues with millions of Americans gathering each year to give their thanks for the same blessings of liberty for which so many brave patriots have laid down their lives to defend during the Revolutionary War and in the years since.

Since the first settlers to call our country home landed on shores, we have always been defined by our resilience and propensity to show gratitude even in the face of great adversity, always remembering the blessings we have been given in spite of the hardships we endure. Thanksgiving, we pause and acknowledge those who will have empty seats at their table. We ask God to watch over our service members, especially those whose selfless commitment to serving our country and defending our sacred liberty has called them to duty overseas during the holiday season. We also pray for our law enforcement officials and first responders as they carry out their duties to protect and serve our communities. Nation, we owe a debt of gratitude to both those who take an oath to safeguard us and our way of life as well as to their families, and we salute them for their immeasurable sacrifices.

As we gather today with those we hold dear, let us give thanks to Almighty God for the many blessings we enjoy. United together as one people, in gratitude for the freedoms and prosperity that thrive across our land, we acknowledge God as the source of all good gifts. We ask Him for protection and wisdom and for opportunities this Thanksgiving to share with others some measure of what we have so providentially received.

Now, therefore, I, Donald J. Trump, President of the United States of America, by virtue of the authority vested in me by the Constitution and the laws of the United States, do hereby proclaim Thursday, November 28, 2019, as a National Day of Thanksgiving. encourage all Americans to gather, in homes and places of worship, to offer a prayer of thanks to God for our many blessings.

In witness whereof, I have hereunto set my hand this twenty-seventh day of November, in the year of our Lord two thousand nineteen, and of the Independence of the United States of America the two hundred and forty-fourth. (Donald Trump, Presidential Proclamation on Thanksgiving Day, 2019)

> But thanks be to God, which giveth us the
> victory through our Lord Jesus Christ.

—1 Corinthians 15:57

Day 6

Anytime we have a feast or celebration, it must come to an end—even if we kept it up for three days of feasting like the pilgrims! As a gathering ends, the work of cleanup has just begun, and so we thought that this poem by Mary Arlis Stuber would fit in here well.

Thank God for Dirty Dishes

Thank God for dirty dishes;
They have a tale to tell.
While others may go hungry,
We're eating very well
With home, health, and happiness,
I shouldn't want to fuss;
By the stack of evidence,
God's been very good to us.

And indeed, he has! Even if it seems like something or everything in your world is not going so well as you read this, I know this will still be true. I know this because God is the same yesterday, today, and forever, and God is good all the time!

Whatever your circumstances and whatever the mess (or lack of mess) before you today, let's thank him, and let's keep on thanking him *every day*!

O give thanks unto the Lord; for he is good:
for his mercy endureth for ever.

—Psalm 136:1

Additional Hymn List

Here is a partial list of some other Thanksgiving Day songs you may want to learn:

1. "All Creatures of Our God and King"
2. "For the Beauty of the Earth"
3. "Give Thanks with a Grateful Heart"
4. "I Will Enter His Gates with Thanksgiving"
5. "Thanks to God for My Redeemer"
6. "To God Be the Glory"
7. "O Let Your Soul Now Be Filled with Gladness"
8. "Jesus, We Just Want to Thank You"

Join our Facebook group: Enter into His presence with Thanksgiving.

About the Author

Daniel and Emily Myers have been married for ten years and have been blessed with six children. They live in Southwest, Missouri, on a small farm, where by the grace of God, they are striving to raise their children to know and love the Lord. They enjoy studying the Bible and singing together as a family. They started writing this book as a way to help their own family focus on being thankful during the holiday season leading up to Thanksgiving Day. Daniel, a chef by trade, has used his artistic talents not only for drawing but also for award-winning ice carvings, window murals, and wood burning. In addition to writing, Emily is a midwife and homeschools their children.